I'M NO TZADDIK

CONFESSIONS
of a
GABBAI

IRVING JACOB

All rights reserved. No part of this publication may be reproduced, distributed, or transmitted in any form or by any means, including photocopying, recording, or other electronic or mechanical methods, without the prior written permission of the publisher, except in the case of brief quotations embodied in critical reviews and certain other noncommercial uses permitted by copyright law.

©2025 Copyright Irving Jacob

Printed in the United States of America

This book is dedicated to the following couples who have allowed me to come over Friday night for Shabbos dinner so I would not have to be alone on Friday night:

Rabbi Nachi and Michelle Klein
David and Peggy Yeager
Bruce and Rena Sandler
Rabbi Eli and Shoshana Rivka Bloom
Toly and Elvira Begelfer
Moti and Soraya Leiter
Mel and Carol Maller
Joel and Rachel Seidel

A special dedication to Rabbi Yosef Maller, my learning partner for over 17 years, for his encouragement to continue learning Gemara

CONTENTS

CHAPTER 1
What is a Gabbai?..7

CHAPTER 2
Aliyahs, Leading Davening, and Fashion......................11

CHAPTER 3
Stand By..17

CHAPTER 4
Let's Go Back to the Beginning: I Come from Somewhere.. 23

CHAPTER 5
Punctuality 55

CHAPTER 6
Waiting...61

CHAPTER 7
Walking to Shul in Hot Weather 65

CHAPTER 8
A Story My Father Told Me 69

CHAPTER 9
A Letter for the Ages 73

CHAPTER 10
Lashon Hara 77

CHAPTER 11
Arlene 81

Epilog 93

About the Author 95

CHAPTER 1

WHAT IS A GABBAI?

Before I answer what a gabbai is, let's' first ask "What is a tzaddik?" A tzaddik is a righteous person according to Jewish standards. He is a righteous man who complies with the moral principles of Judaism. Although I try to be an observant Jew, I wish I was a tzaddik. However, I keep trying to get there. A righteous woman is called a tzedekes.

In earlier times the gabbai was a treasurer or honorary official of an Orthodox Jewish congregation. He often was placed in charge of charity funds.[1] In ancient times the gabbaim (plural for gabbai) were men who gathered taxes for the Roman government. Although their reputations were beyond reproach, the Talmud requires that they work in pairs to avoid suspicion of wrongdoing. The Talmud reads "We may have no less than seven supervisors and three treasurers. And no financial authority may be established over the public (consisting of) less than two (officials).[2]

Today a gabbai is someone who assists with the Torah reading. When the Torah is taken out to be read in the synagogue, one man reads the Torah while being flanked on both sides by the gabbaim who ensure that the Torah is being read correctly. In fact, one of the gabbaim will give various hand signals at the request of the reader to help him sing the correct trope. One of the gabbaim assigns *aliyahs* to seven different men to be called up to the Torah. He calls them up in order of those to be honored with an *aliyah*.

The other duties include keeping the rabbi informed, enforcing the rabbi's directives, greeting new people who come into the shul, and making sure that synagogue services run smoothly. This includes assigning various men to lead various parts of the weekday, Shabbos, and Yontiv services.

---

[1] www.brotannica.com/topic/gabbai
[2] Talmud tractate Shekalim, Artscroll, Chapter 5, Mishna 2, p. 14 b1, Mesorah Publications

In addition, the gabbai is responsible for assigning a man to take *Maftir* (*Haftarah*) on Shabbos, Yontiv, and on fast days. In my job as gabbai I try always to remember to act with reverence because this is the work of heaven.[3] Thus, the gabbai also has the role of stage manager. In the times of our sages three gabbaim were appointed for the shul. In current times they are either appointed or elected by the shul members. In my shul the gabbai rishon (first gabbai) and gabbai Sheini (second gabbai) are elected. Also, current gabbaim for the most part, with few exceptions, take no charge over money. Shuls usually have a treasurer and/or financial secretary to handle these matters.

The gabbai sheini assists the gabbai rishon at the Torah reader's desk. He helps to correct mistakes and assumes the gabbai rishon's duty in the latter's absence (appointing leaders of davening and calling up those to the Torah who have been given aliyahs). Upon the gabbai rishon's return, he resumes the duties once more.

---

3   Schpektor, Rabbi David Awraham, Sefer HaGabbai, p. 24, The Hebron Rabbinical Research Institute

CHAPTER 2

ALIYAHS, LEADING DAVENING, AND FASHION

When calling up those for an aliyah, the order is a follows: First aliyah: Kohen (from the tribe of Levi whose ancestry is of the priests). Second aliyah: Levi (also of the tribe of Levi whose ancestry is of the Levites). Third aliyah: Yisroel (the common man). Fourth aliyah: Yisroel.

Fifth aliyah: Yisroel. Sixth aliyah: Yisroel. Seventh aliyah: Yisroel. The Maftir can be given to a Kohen, Levy, or Yisroel. According to Rabbi Schpektor, if there is no Kohen, a Levy can be called up for the first aliyah in an Ashkenazic shul.[4]

However, in 2016 I attended a gabbai seminar at Congregation Beth Jacob in Los Angeles. The featured speaker was Rabbi Herschel Schacter. A gabbai asked him if a Levy can be called up first in the absence of a Kohen. Rabbi Schacter answered that it's not forbidden, but not proper. I have been instructed by my rabbi[5] not to call up a Levy in the absence of a Kohen. Instead, a Yisroel is to be called up throughout the Torah reading.

Rabbi Moishe Dovid Lebovitz writes that one should not daven without socks even if he is wearing slippers, clogs, or Crocs.[6] However, during the week I allow one to lead davening and to be given an aliyah if not wearing socks as long as their shoes are closed. If one wears open shoes without socks, I won't let him daven from the amud nor give him an aliyah.

The same thing will be said for shorts. Rabbi Schacter said at the gabbai seminar that no one in shorts is to be allowed to daven from the amud. He said "absolutely under

---

[4] Ibid., p. 145
[5] Rabbi Nachi Klein, Young Israel of Northridge
[6] Lebovitz, Rabbi Moishe Dovid, Halachically Speaking, p. 66, Israel Book Shop Publications, Lakewood, NJ

no circumstances." A gabbai asked him what would be if this individual has an obligation due to being in mourning or having a yahrzeit. Rabbi Schacter repeated "absolutely under no circumstances."

At one time I forgot to check what a man was wearing before I called him up for an aliyah. When I called him up, I saw that he wore shorts. I wanted to direct him back to his seat, but a rabbi said that since I already called him up, he needs to have the aliyah. From then on I always have checked to see what one wears before calling him up for an aliyah or before having him daven from the amud.

I used to wear shorts to shul on weekdays during the summer months, but ceased to do so in 2003. Although wearing shorts is not forbidden for a man, I began to feel that it wasn't proper. And besides, while in shorts, I couldn't daven from the amud. Currently on the weekdays I wear a polo shirt and Dockers to shul as this is the accepted dress. Some men also wear jeans. I wear jeans on Sunday and Friday with three exceptions. They are Yontiv, Chol Hamoed, and Rosh Chodesh. On Shabbos and Yontiv, as well as on other occasions such as weddings, I wear a suit, tie, and a black hat.

When a gabbai chooses one to daven from the amud or gives him an aliyah, a worshipper might feel insulted due to thinking that he was overlooked. Rabbi Schpektor writes that if a worshipper feels insulted, he must overcome his feelings and say nothing to him in this regard.[7] However, a gabbai might have forgotten to give someone an aliyah when it was promised to him. If such is the case, he should make it up to him and give him an aliyah at the first available opportunity. The same goes for choosing one to daven from the amud.

Years ago during a prior term as gabbai I forgot to give someone an aliyah who was sponsoring Kiddush that Shabbos. In our shul it's a custom to give such a man an aliyah or Haftarah. When the man's cousin approached me, he said that I failed to give him an aliyah for sponsoring Kiddush. I then realized that I totally forgot about it and felt bad. I proceeded to promise it to him at Mincha (afternoon service) and followed through with it. Both men appreciated my making up for the mistake.

On the other hand, if one wants an aliyah or the Haftarah, he needs to ask the gabbai. He cannot assume that the gabbai knows to give these. Usually the Kiddush sponsor is happy to receive an aliyah. I experienced a such incident twice. I knew who sponsored Kiddush at both Shabosos and gave them aliyahs. They refused to go up. Each thought they would get the Haftarah. The rabbi offered to help and

---

[7] Schpektor, Rabbi David Awraham, op. cit., p. 38.

asked if the men chosen for the Haftarahs could relinquish the honor. They were gracious enough to relinquish, Baruch Hashem. This is what can happen if one doesn't ask the gabbai for a specific honor and just assumes that he will be given it. Many of us know what assume means; (*blank*) of you and me.

At the same time, the gabbai should ask the Kiddush sponsor if he would like to have the Haftarah (if he is capable). If not, the gabbai then should offer him an aliyah. Lesson learned.

If the gabbai has made a mistake and has called up the wrong man, the worshipper should try not to feel insulted. The gabbai often is in a tough spot and needs to make a quick decision. He cannot take too much time to decide who gets what honor. Example: when the time comes for the *hagbah* (one who lifts the Torah) and *gelihah* (one who closes the Torah) to go up, the gabbai must have specific men in mind before calling them up. Taking too much time to decide who will do these can create *tiercha al hatzibbur* (strain on the community).

CHAPTER 3

STAND BY

Rabbi Schpektor writes that the gabbai should not initiate a new shul custom without asking the shul rabbi.[8] Well, without intending to, I started one. In the mornings before davening time I say "Stand by" three minutes and one minute before the start time. Thus, at 6:57 A.M. and 6:59 A.M. weekdays and 8:27 A.M and 8:29 A.M. on Shabbos I call out "Stand by." At 7:00 A.M. weekdays and 8:30 A.M. Shabbos I slap the reader's desk to signal the

---

8 Ibid., p. 36

start time. When the rabbi was present at one of these calls, he said "This is a shul, not a TV studio." With that I learned not to say it in his presence. Also, I learned not to slap the reader's desk in the rabbi's presence.

Where did the practice of saying stand by originate? There was a time when television stations did not broadcast around the clock. They would broadcast from the early afternoon until Midnight. In order to let the viewer know that the channel was working, a test pattern was displayed on the screen and accompanied by a testing noise.

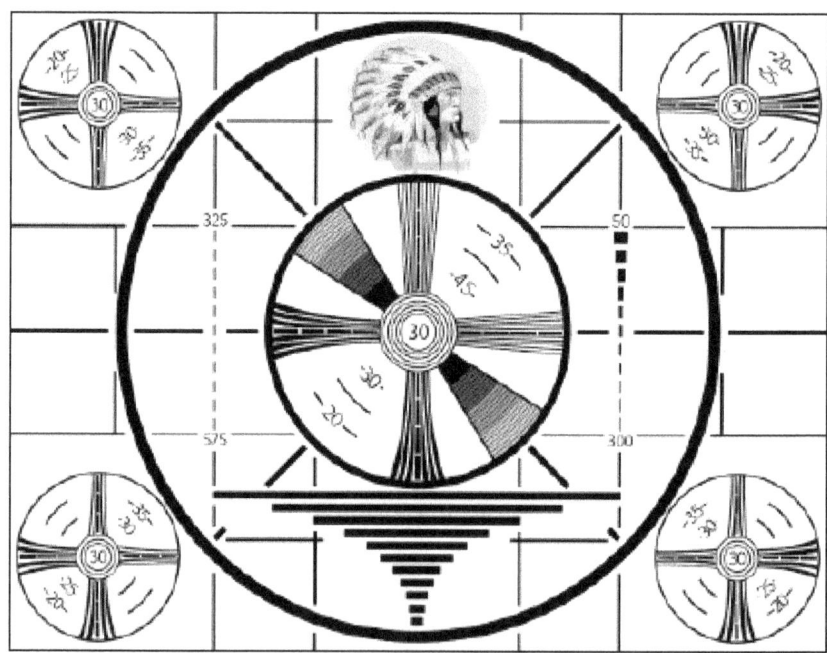

Early day television test pattern

Old televisions had knobs to adjust vertical and horizontal beam synchronization. This way one could tell if a problem existed. Sometimes it was necessary to move the antenna around (in many cases more than just sometimes). The pattern was meant to make various distortions, ghosting, and echoes easy to spot.[9]

When the television network was interrupted, either the picture or sound would disappear (sometimes both). A few minutes later an announcer would say "Please stand by" in order to tell the viewers that the engineers were working on the problem. Most of the time the interruption was five minutes and at other times the interruption could be for a half hour. As a child I always got very upset if a program I liked was interrupted.

During a childhood visit to a TV studio there was a red light and green light on the wall. When the red light was on, a sign read Stand By. When the green light was on, a sign read On The Air. Also, someone would call out Stand By several times before the program went on the air. During the standby there was to be no talking prior to going on the air and definitely no talking when the program went on the air.

---

9 https://www.reddit.com/r/AskHistorians/comments/46 yevi/what_are_the_origins_of_the_classoc_please_stand

At the shul I say "Stand By" in the mornings only. The mornings begin the day and I say "Stand By' to indicate that the day is beginning and we need to wake up. I don't say it at Mincha because the day is winding down. On other days I do not say it due to the gravity of the day…Rosh Hashanah, Yom Kippur, Tisha B'Av, and Hoshanah Rabbah. I'll explain in the last chapter why I don't say it on Hoshanah Rabbah.

When the rabbi is not around, I say "Stand By" at the usual three minutes and one minute prior to starting the davening. Immediately thereafter someone will ask "which One?" I say "…the second one. At the next one when asked which one, I say the first one. Thus, the second one comes before the first one. One morning when the rabbi came in a few minutes early, I said jokingly that this wasn't fair. He then said that he would stand outside so I could say it. After 6:59 A.M. he came into the shul.

Also, when I went out of town, the gabbai sheini asked me to record the words on WhatsApp. When I recorded the words, he played them on his cellphone at the normal times and the rabbi laughed. On a visit to the Miami Beach Community Kollel I said "Stand by" to see how the men would react. They looked at me in a peculiar fashion of surprise. My son, who lives in Miami Beach and heard me call out "Stand By," said that I should just as well say "Squirrel."

Some of the men in the shul don't like it and I won't say it in their presence. But for now, shul is beginning. STAND BY.

CHAPTER 4

LET'S GO BACK TO THE BEGINNING:
I Come from Somewhere

I was born in Dallas, Texas in 1948 just a year after my parents came to America from Shanghai, China after World War II. They had escaped Germany in 1939 and found refuge in Shanghai. Years later my mother told me that while in Shanghai the rabbi permitted the community to eat rice on Pesach. After all, this was war and there was a food shortage with rice being one of the few plentiful crops.

I grew up Conservative. At home we kept Pesach, the High Holy Days, and Chanukah. My mother grew up in an Orthodox home and my father didn't. When they married in Shanghai, my mother gave up the kosher home not to restore it upon her arrival to America.

When I was four years old, my parents enrolled me in the kindergarten under the auspices of the United Hebrew Schools in south Dallas. Here I learned many of the Jewish customs including Chanukah, Purim, the High Holy Days, and Pesach. Each year my mother made beautiful Seders.

At the time south Dallas was the Jewish area until the Jews moved north in the mid 50's. My parents attended Congregation Shearith Israel… the Conservative shul of south Dallas. The most known Orthodox shul was Agudas Achim. The United Hebrew Schools was the result of a merger in 1946 of the Hebrew School of Dallas with Hertze Chaikel Talmud Torah of Agudas Achim.[10]

In 1956 Congregation Shearith Israel built a new building in the north part of Dallas on Douglas Ave at Walnut Hill Lane. This building would house a synagogue and

---

10 Biderman, Rose G., They Came to Stay, p. 159, Eakin Press, Division of Sunbelt Media, Inc., Austin, TX.

Hebrew school which would meet three days a week. Here Shearith Israel merged with the United Hebrew Schools and thus the United Hebrew schools ceased to exist as an independent entity. When I was six, I attended Sunday school in the old Shearith Israel building for two years. Here we learned Biblical stories in a way that children could understand.

In 1956 Shearith Israel moved to the new building on Douglas Ave at Walnut Hill Lane. I was eight at the time and was assigned to attend Hebrew school three times a week (Sunday, Tuesday, and Thursday). On Tuesday and Thursday, I would attend after regular school. The Sunday session went from 10:45 A.M. until 12:30 P.M. while the Tuesday and Thursday sessions went from 4:00 to 6:00 P.M. Other kids were assigned to attend Sunday, Monday, and Wednesday. The Sunday session went from 9:00 A.M. until 10:45 A.M. while the Monday and Wednesday sessions were at the same time as the Tuesday and Thursday sessions.

During most of the first year of Hebrew School we still lived close to south Dallas although most of the Jewish community was gone from there. The new Jewish neighborhood was in the nicer north part. Therefore, my parents drove quite a distance (11 miles) to get me to Hebrew school and back home. However, in April, 1957 we moved to the north part, making the distance to Shearith Israel only three miles.

I didn't like going to Hebrew school. I felt that the atmosphere was very stuffy. My dislike was reflected on my first report card (given at Chanukah) which was quite poor. A few months later I was transferred to another class which I liked better and my attitude toward Hebrew school changed for the better. This was reflected in much better report cards (given at Purim and in June when the Hebrew school broke for the summer). In the United Hebrew Schools we said prayers with the Ashkenazic pronunciation. However, in the Hebrew school at Shearith Israel the policy was to say the prayers with the Sephardic pronunciation. Thus, for many years I said the prayers in the latter style. The rabbi at the time followed the ruling of the conservative movement and required the prayers in the synagogue to be in the Sephardic pronunciation.

On Saturday the junior congregation services were held in other rooms from the synagogue areas. For my first year of Hebrew School I didn't attend because I never thought much of it and I didn't know about Shabbos as this wasn't practiced at home.

The second year of Hebrew school I began attending the junior congregation services. The rabbi and board of directors bribed us to come by calling us up on the pulpit for the monthly honor roll if we came the whole month. If we were called up six to eight times in the year, we would get a small trophy. If we were called up nine or ten times, we would get a big trophy. I didn't get on the honor roll enough to receive a trophy but in my third year I was on the honor roll nine times and got a large plaque.

One Saturday night I attended a pre-teen and teenage function in the synagogue. Before the function began, we did Havdalah. When they passed around the spices, the spice box came to me and I asked "What do I do with it?" The advisor explained to me that I am to smell it. So I did.

At 13 I was Bar Mitzvah and this was a highlight of my life at that time. I enjoyed the attention that I got on that day. I then graduated Hebrew school and went into pre confirmation class. One was required to be in pre confirmation before going the next year to the confirmation class.

These classes met on Shabbos and Sunday. On Shabbos we would attend class and then go to the synagogue area for the Musaph service. We couldn't hear the Torah reading as we were in class with facts being thrown at us. The class was quite academic and I had a hard time competing with the other students.

At the same time I played in the band at my middle school (called junior high school back then). Since I was in the marching band, some of the rehearsals were on Saturdays and I was required to be there. Thus, the Jewish life and band life could not co-exist. Since some of these rehearsals also were on Saturday morning, I therefore had to miss some pre confirmation and confirmation class sessions.

At the end of the year we were given tests to see if we passed pre confirmation in order to go to the confirmation class. Of course, I failed and was told that I would need to repeat pre confirmation. I begged for another chance and the chance was given to me. I had to write a paper for my pre confirmation teacher and if it passed, I could go on to the confirmation class. My paper passed.

In the confirmation class we used the book Pathways Through the Bible by Mortimer J. Cohen. Being the lazy student that I was, I didn't read the assignments but somehow passed the tests by cramming the information the week before. On Shabbos we were in the class from 9:30 A.M. until 11:00 A.M. Afterwards we were taken by our teacher into the shul for the Musaph service.

On Sunday we met from 9:00 A.M. until 11:00 A.M. From 9:00 to 10:00 we were instructed by the rabbi and every week he would present another theme. Little did I know that all these themes would be on our only test from him. This solo test also was our final exam with him. I scored a failing 39. The other final exam was from our main teacher. I passed that one.

The confirmation graduation ceremony took place on the second day of Shavuos. The ceremony usually was on the first day; but, the first day was exam day at the Dallas public schools. Therefore, the conservative shul had the ceremony done on the second day which was dead day in the public schools after all exams were administered. We were dressed in our caps and gowns and marched in procession to the pulpit to have all of our names called. This ceremony occurred every year with all the yearly confirmation classes. Until I got into confirmation class, I didn't know why we celebrated Shavuos. I always thought that it was a holiday to honor the confirmation class. Later, though, I learned that Shavuos commemorates the receiving of the Torah by Moses.

During my year in the confirmation class I joined the Dallas Chapter of the USY (United Synagogue Youth). The USY is the youth movement of the United Synagogue of Conservative Judaism. It was founded in 1951 under the auspices of the Youth Commission of what was then the United Synagogue of America.

In the USY I was one of the least knowledgeable about Judaism but I tried to learn. I slowly began to attend more functions and my learning increased. My first out of town function was the regional convention in Houston. I met new people and learned more about Judaism. This time I learned about Havdalah and what the spices were for. They were to maintain the sweet aroma of Shabbos as we were ushering Shabbos out.

In fact, I learned more about Judaism in the USY than I leaned in Hebrew school. In fact, although my parents didn't buy into keeping a kosher home, I sometimes was able to influence them to having formal Shabbos meals on Friday nights with Kiddush over wine and Hamotzi for the bread. Also, after attending a national convention in 1963 I was inspired to wear tefillin every morning.

I wanted to observe Shabbos as much as possible, but, still, I was in the high school band; and that was not possible. Although I continued playing in the band, I would attend shul whenever possible. Until I got my driver's license I didn't go to shul in the morning. However, our USY chapter often had the function of attending Shabbos Mincha. Here I learned about davening the Mincha (afternoon) and Maariv (night) services. Also, the Havdalah service was more ingratiated in me. This time I knew what to do when the spices came around to me.

After graduating from confirmation class, I decided to continue my Jewish education at the shul and entered three years of post confirmation. This time there were no tests. We just sat (as in seminar style) and participated in discussions about Judaism. In the third year the teacher was Orthodox and he influenced me a great deal. I was a senior in high school and he encouraged me to apply to Yeshiva University in New York for the following year.

Yeshiva University rejected me due to insufficient grades. I ended up attending the University of North Texas as a music major with a concentration in percussion. I played in the marching band and some of the games were on Shabbos afternoon. However, most of the games were on Saturday night. While there I lived in the dormitory and obviously was not kosher. However, I avoided pork. The next semester I applied to Yeshiva University again and was rejected a second time. After my first full year I applied again and even was granted an interview at Yeshiva University. However, I was rejected a third time.

At 16 I passed the driving test for my driver's license. With my license I drove to shul as much as possible while in high school and home from college. When there was no Bar Mitzvah, the gabbai sometimes gave me an aliyah. The gabbai was Mr. Abe Jacobs. To this day I haven't known a gabbai like him. How he kept control in a shul of often 500 people is beyond me. The 1959 Shearith Israel diamond anniversary book described him this way: "Abe H. Jacobs, associate gabbai for almost 25 years, has been an important link in the transmission of our sacred heritage."

Although Mr. Jacobs gave me an aliyah on Shabbos morning, he never gave me one in the afternoon at Shabbos Mincha. I once said to him that he never gave me one during Shabbos Mincha after two years of attending. He replied in his Texas accent "Well that's too bad. I've been coming here every morning and evening for 33 years and I ain't gotten one yet." That shut my mouth in a hurry. So much for a 17-year-old making inappropriate comments and being ungrateful to boot. Abe Jacobs was gabbai of the shul from 1934 until his passing in 1977. To repeat, to this day I have yet to find a gabbai of his caliber.

During my second year at the University of North Texas I was accepted to the Conservative Jewish university in Los Angeles. The acceptance letter came in March, 1968 and the new school year would begin in September of that year. I intended to study sacred music and for the Conservative rabbinate after being influenced by the USY and my third year post confirmation instructor.

From then until the end of the summer, 1968 year at the University of North Texas my non Jewish girl friend and I broke up since I told her that I would spend the following school year in Los Angeles. Also, the people at the university were not supportive. I met with much teasing about my wanting to study to be a rabbi.

On September 11, 1968 I arrived in Los Angeles (sight unseen). From the airport I was picked up and driven to the Conservative Jewish university on Sunset Blvd. When I got there, the head of the fine arts department introduced himself to me and took me to his office to discuss the curriculum. In addition to the curriculum we discussed the tuition.

When I went to the Hebrew department, I was introduced to the department head and we discussed the Hebrew classes that I would take. The program sounded difficult and he replied "At this stage of the game you will need to learn all the Hebrew you can because the upper level classes are no longer conducted in English. They're conducted in Hebrew." Right then and there I felt that something would not work out.

The two classes in which the instructors were supportive were the religion and Biblical cantillations classes. The remaining classes were not supportive. They talked to us as if we were five-year-old children. After some weeks the Hebrew instructor yelled at us saying that we were not progressing.

Also, in the music theory/ composition class we were to compose Shabbos evening works for the cantors and choirs. When I showed the instructor my work, he demanded to know why I didn't write a part for the organ. I replied that I didn't believe in the organ being used in shul. He snapped "You're an ignoramus. Eighty percent of the Conservative shuls in Los Angeles use organs. So you better get used to it." With that I was completely turned off to Judaism. In the following spring semester I enrolled at California State University Northridge (then San Fernando Valley State College). Also, in the spring semester due to the lack of support and loss of inspiration, I stopped wearing tefillin.

On a short visit to Dallas in February, 1969 I met with the Shearith Israel rabbi who asked how I was doing at the Conservative Jewish university. I explained to him that I always thought that I wanted to be a rabbi; but, after my experience at the Conservative university, I said that I didn't want to be a rabbi. He replied "Irving, I never wanted to discourage you because I thought you knew what you wanted. But, I would want to discourage my son from being a rabbi."

I further said to the rabbi that I didn't like the use of an organ in the shul and I hoped that he would fight to his last breath to keep it out of here. He replied "Don't worry. We won't get one. Nobody wants it. We don't want to be drowned out in our singing by an organ. We will stick to the acapella style."

On Shabbos in Los Angeles I attended the Conservative shul almost two miles away from the Conservative university. Since we had no large student group staying over for Shabbos, it was up to us to attend shul on our own. The shul used an organ. But, since I didn't have many options as to where to attend, I settled for this particular shul. Occasionally the shul rabbi invited me to his house for Shabbos lunch.

At Cal State Northridge I resumed my education as a music major with my concentration as a percussionist. I played in the symphonic wind ensemble and in the secondary band. Concerts were on Friday night, but I didn't care. I enjoyed performing and was excited about the following year to play in the marching band. As far as attending the synagogue, I could be considered one of those three-day Jews which means going only on Rosh Hashanah and Yom Kippur. However, I occasionally attended the late Friday night services at some of the Conservative shuls. And yes, they used organs. That I didn't like, but I knew of no Conservative shuls which didn't use these. And yes, I drove to shul and back home on Friday nights.

In addition to being a percussionist I studied conducting and occasionally got to conduct. I composed a work for percussion ensemble which I conducted at a Friday night spring concert. Also, in the following year I was given the opportunity to conduct the percussion ensemble in one piece at another concert and was given the opportunity to conduct the university orchestra during the orchestra class.

I graduated with a Bachelor of Arts degree in 1970 and continued with graduate work. In 1972 I earned my Master of Arts degree in music. After I received my MA degree, I took additional music classes and began rewriting a 40-page paper (topic was the development of the marimba) that I wrote for the research techniques class in graduate school. Originally I received a B on the paper, but the professor said that it was awkward.

After rewriting the paper I resubmitted it to the professor to see if he now though that it was suitable for publication. He said that he thought the paper was still awkward. With that I gave the paper a few months thought and began rewriting it a second time. This time I didn't resubmit it to the professor. Instead, I submitted the paper to the editor of The Percussionist magazine and he accepted it for publication.

A few months later when the magazine printed the first section of the paper, I made a copy and placed it in some of the professors' boxes, including the research techniques professor. A few days later when we passed each other in the hall, he smiled and said, "Thanks for the article and congratulations." In a later meeting with other professors he said that he never thought that there would be enough material to write a 40-page paper on the development of the marimba and have it published.

After having received my MA degree in 1972, I also was accepted to perform in the Ventura Symphony Orchestra, the Mount Community Orchestra, and the Santa Monica Symphony orchestra. My stay with Ventura lasted until 1974. My stay with the Santa Monica Symphony Orchestra lasted until 1976 and with the Mount Community Orchestra until 1977. Also, from 1973 until 1975 I was the assistant conductor of the Santa Monica Youth Orchestra. The latter rehearsals were Saturday mornings.

Teaching jobs were scarce during this time. Thus, I was unable to find a teaching job in music at the college level. Therefore, since I needed to survive economically, I took a job as a shipping clerk at a small manufacturing company.

I worked some overtime to make more money and occasionally worked on Saturdays.

In 1973 I attended High Holy Day services (Rosh Hashanah and Yom Kippur) at the Cal State Northridge Hillel House. For the first time in several years I felt inspired and wanted to return to my Jewish roots. After all the Holy Days were over, the Hillel director announced the Jewish Outreach group. This was in the form of an encounter group which I decided to attend.

The encounter group was a weekly session of people who were trying to find their Jewish roots and who wanted to obtain self-improvement. After a few sessions I failed to feel the support that I thought I would get. People began to say that I was a phony and I just couldn't believe that I was hearing this. When they tried to get me to talk, I just couldn't get any words out. After all the scolding and not feeling safe, I dropped out of the group and was once again turned off to Judaism.

In 1974 after I began working as a shipping clerk, I again searched for something Jewish, but didn't want anything particularly religious. I was told of a Jewish social organization in the Valley whose members were between 21 and 35 years of age. I decided to attend a Saturday night party which I enjoyed enough to want to attend their monthly meeting a few weeks later. Eventually I became increasingly involved.

Several of the social group's functions were on Saturday; but, I just was looking for a Jewish group. Many times, though, they held creative Shabbos services on Friday night which I attended and enjoyed. In addition to this social group, I found out about the Jewish co-op in Northridge. Some Jewish students lived there and they had Shabbos meals every Friday night. For almost a year I attended these events pretty regularly.

In 1975 during my involvement with the social group, I also rejoined the Jewish Outreach at the Cal State Northridge Hillel House. To my good fortune, the 1973 group was gone and I felt safe. This was an outgrowth of the Cal State Northridge Hillel group. The Jewish Outreach group was for people who were older than college age. The outreach split up into different smaller groups and I joined one of them.

Later on the outreach group organized the Bayit on Friday nights. I opted to attend these each Friday night as long as the other social group had no Friday night function. And, although these groups were not religious, they influenced me to stop dating non-Jewish girls. From 1975 onward I dated only Jewish girls and never looked back.

In 1975 I again attended High Holy Day services at the Cal State Northridge Hillel House. The rabbi was Rabbi Ben Zion Levin [Ala Hasholom (May he rest in peace in Hebrew)], affectionately known as Rabbi Ben. He was an Orthodox Hillel director and thus did the service in the Orthodox way. I couldn't handle it. I didn't care for the mechizah (partition separating men and women). I never had experienced that in my life. After the Holy Days were over, I left the Hillel House until the non-religious outreach group reconvened. I never introduced myself to Rabbi Levin.

In 1976 I felt that I had outgrown the original social group and left them in order to devote all my time to the Jewish Outreach and the Friday night Bayit. Although the group was not particularly religious, I felt that I was getting more of the Judaism that I was searching for. The headquarters was the Hillel House, but we met at different people's homes. The Bayit, though, met at the apartment of the one in charge.

In 1976 I attended the High Holy Day services again at the Hillel House and again lead by Rabbi Ben. This time I formally introduced myself to him. He welcomed me warmly. I still, though, was not used to the Orthodox way of davening.

In October, 1976 while attending the Friday night Bayit, the leader told me that Rabbi Ben needed me for the minyan (quorum of 10 men) the next morning at the Hillel House. I decided that I had nothing to lose and I would go. While there I felt very awkward since it had been a long time since I had attended a Shabbos morning service.

I thought that since I helped once to make the minyan, I wouldn't be called again. But, the following Friday night at the Bayit, the leader said that Rabbi Ben needed me. I reluctantly went. However, this time I got accustomed to the davening and I enjoyed the service. I no longer was bothered by the mechizah. I also attended regularly each Shabbos morning without having to be notified by the Bayit leader.

Between the Orthodox Shabbos minyan and the Jewish Outreach involvement, I became more involved with Judaism. From here I became more traditional. In fact, in the spring 1977 semester at Cal State Northridge I took a class in Jewish Identity in the United States. The Jewish professor was not religious, but saw that I wanted to be more traditional. She thus encouraged me to go that way. I got a B in the class.

The Rabbi Ben minyan struggled to stay afloat since we didn't always have at least 10 men. We competed with the traditional minyan at the Conservative synagogue. These men originally were part of the Hillel minyan but left to form the traditional minyan. Shortly before Pesach 1977 the Rabbi Ben minyan was disbanded. However, I was invited for the first night Pesach Seder at Rabbi Ben's house. On the second night I was at the house of one of the Rabbi Ben minyan members.

I had no other choice but to attend the traditional minyan if I didn't want to daven alone. I joined them for Pesach and then became a regular on Shabbos morning. Just as in the Rabbi Ben minyan, here too, I got to occasionally lead the davening. This minyan did not have a mechizah; but, for a while the women sat behind the men's section.

I didn't take off work on Yontiv if it fell on weekdays except for Rosh Hashanah and Yom Kippur. I still didn't want to possibly alienate my work colleagues and supervisors. Still, though, when Yontiv fell on Shabbos and Sunday, I was in shul. With my being inspired by Rabbi Ben and the Jewish Identity class at Cal State Northridge, I began wearing tefillin again in May, 1977.

In the fall of 1977 I heard that Rabbi Ben was starting up the Hillel minyan again on Shabbos and the High Holy Days. I gladly abandoned the traditional minyan for a while and rejoined the Hillel minyan. In fact, Rabbi Ben had me lead part of the High Holy Day davening. After the High Holy Days we continued to have Shabbos davening at the Hillel House.

In November, 1977 Rabbi Ben organized an in-Shabbos at the Hillel House. He invited us from the minyan and the students and faculty from Yeshiva University of Los Angeles (YULA). This was a very inspirational Shabbos as we learned about Shir Hashirim (Song of Songs) on that Friday night. The next morning we davened and did some learning prior to the Kiddush and lunch.

During the lunch I sat across from one of the YULA rabbis. He asked me about my religiosity. I explained that I observe Shabbos as best I can. He asked if I drive on Shabbos. I answered "just to the shul and back home." Although driving is not allowed on Shabbos, this, for me, was a step forward as I stopped driving to other places and ceased doing errands and shopping. Still, the YULA rabbi was supportive and didn't judge me.

A few weeks later I took a trip to Israel to get more acquainted with my Jewish roots. The most beautiful experience was to daven at the Western Wall. I felt very elevated to daven with my tefillin and then again to daven at night at the wall.

In early 1978 the Hillel minyan disbanded once again. Although the minyan disbanded, I kept in touch with Rabbi

Ben until he moved to Connecticut to take a pulpit. I then returned to the traditional minyan at the Conservative shul. I lead davening and did some of the Haftarahs. And again, although there was no mechizah, the men sat in front and the women either sat in the middle or rear section. However, sometime later a lady came into the minyan and sat in the front with the men. This time it bothered me. I then realized how much I had grown Jewishly. After this lady sat in front with the men, other women followed suit and did the same.

Also In the spring 1978 semester I took a class in American Jewish history at the Conservative Jewish university. We covered subjects of how the European Jews immigrated to America beginning in the 1880's. At that time most European immigrants were unmarried males. The majority of immigration by families began at the turn of the century. Other topics covered were the jobs that the immigrants had in America. From here came the topic of the sweatshops.

The professor had to dismiss the class before the official semester concluded due to heading a Pesach cruise. He gave us our final exams prior to his leaving. There were 10 essay questions and we were to choose eight of the 10 ten questions to answer. He required a minimum of 25 pages. We wrote the answers in pen because at that time desktop computers were not a common item. I came up with 25 pages and got a B in the class.

During this time I switched from davening in the Sephardic pronunciation to the Ashkenazic pronunciation. Through this I returned to my old roots from kindergarten where we were taught prayers in the Ashkenazic style. I figured that since I'm an Ashkenazic Jew, I also should daven the Ashkenazic way; and I have maintained this practice ever since.

In spring 1978 I began to have formal Shabbos evening meals at home. Before this time, I only had these Friday evening meals with the Jewish co-op. Now I was ready to set up my table for Shabbos. Also, in 1978 I began wearing tzitzis (fringes).

Shortly before Shavuos 1978 I was invited to an in-Shabbos at YULA which I gladly attended. This in-Shabbos had all the yeshiva students there. We davened Friday night and did Kiddush afterwards. A lavish meal followed. Following the meal we danced and listened to various Torah lectures.

After all was over that night, most students went to bed. However, in my room, my roommate and I with others, stayed up and talked until 1:30 A.M. Believe it or not, I still got up in time for the morning davening. As a side note, my roommate (Ken Kaufman) at the in Shabbos was someone I knew from the traditional minyan in Northridge.

After the morning davening we did Kiddush and then had our meal. Eating and singing were the order of the meal. Later the rabbi gave a devar Torah. Afterwards we went to our rooms to nap and then returned for Mincha. I got to lead the Mincha and felt elated to do this at a yeshiva.

After Shabbos the rabbis, who asked about my religiosity at the Cal State Northridge in-Shabbos in November, 1977, invited me to apply to YULA for learning. I explained that I had been rejected three times by Yeshiva University in New York. He said that now that I had graduated college, this wouldn't matter. I thus applied in 1978 and was accepted. This acceptance made me feel vindicated after three rejections from New York. However, I was unable to attend due to finances.

In summer 1978 I changed my apartment to kosher. I wanted to keep a kosher home months earlier, but my roommate at the time was not favorable toward it. Although my apartment wasn't kosher, I bought only kosher meat to bring home since fall 1977. In summer 1978 my roommate moved out and I was able to keep the kosher home that I wanted. I changed the dishes and Rabbi Joshua Gordon of Chabad (Ala Hasholom) made my oven kosher.

Now that I was more entrenched in my Judaism, I told my bosses that I wouldn't work Shabbos. However, I offered to come in on an occasional Sunday if necessary. This proposition was accepted and I did just that. However, I still only took off for Rosh Hashanah and Yom Kippur and I still only took off the other Holy Days if they fell weekends.

Although I kept a kosher home, I still ate meat out. I still enjoyed the fried chicken at Shakey's Pizza and the big hamburgers at the non-kosher restaurants. However, in January, 1979, while engaged to Arlene, I decided that if I'm kosher at home, I need to be kosher out. I gave up eating meat at non-kosher restaurants.

In November, 1982 I left the traditional minyan at the Northridge Conservative shul as I looked for a more religious environment. I then decided to go to the Chabad of the Valley in Encino where a mechizah was. At that time I still drove to shul, but I refrained from all other prohibited activities. I enjoyed the welcoming environment.

In December, 1982 I received a call from one of the guys who was involved in the Rabbi Ben minyan at the Cal State Northridge Hillel House. He asked me if I would be interested to help start an Orthodox shul in Northridge. Without hesitation I said yes emphatically. He proceeded to say that the goal was to have our first Shabbos davening on January 22, 1983. I said that I would be there.

Arlene was not too keen on the idea of an Orthodox shul as she was not observant at the time. She thought that it was enough for her to keep a kosher home for me. She preferred the Conservative shul traditional minyan. While there I had decided to sit with her only and with no other women. But I later realized that I no longer felt right about it.

On Shabbos, January 23, 1983 our first Shabbos minyan got off the ground. We davened at the guest house of Ralph Alpert (alav v'sholom) and we had exactly 10 men. Believe it or not, the one who called me didn't come because he thought that there wouldn't be a minyan since it was raining. But, sure enough, we had the minyan and we davened. And to boot, I walked to shul for the first time on that Shabbos. I did this from then on. Ralph Alpert was the major mover for starting the shul.

We originally tried to go under the auspices of Chabad, but they wouldn't take us. They felt that there were not enough Orthodox Jews in Northridge to justify having anything here. We then tried Yeshiva University, but they declined us. The third try was the National Council of Young Israel. They took us. We then became the Young Israel of Northridge.

We didn't think that we were ready to have High Holy Day services that year. But, a few months later we decided to have them. The turnout was quite successful. I hoped that Arlene would attend with me; but, she decided to go to the services put on by the Cal State Northridge Hillel which no longer was Orthodox since Rabbi Ben had left.

Between Rosh Hashanah and Yom Kippur 1983 I went to an Orthodox shul in North Hollywood on Sunday morning since the Young Israel of Northridge shul couldn't yet get a commitment of enough men for the weekday davening. When I got to the North Hollywood shul, I saw through the window what I thought were men doing psalms before the regular weekday services. When someone came out, I asked what was going on. He said that they were doing Selichos (penitential) services since we still were in the 10 days of repentance. I thought that Selichos were done only on the Saturday night prior to Rosh Hashanah. The man was nice enough to explain to me that Selichos are done beginning on the Saturday night prior to Rosh Hashanah but are also done each day between Rosh Hashanah and Yom Kippur except on Shabbos. This is what I had not yet learned. The next year, though, I purchased a Selichos book in order to do all the daily Selichos between Rosh Hashanah and Yom Kippur.

In 1984 I went public with my yarmulke. I decided that I now would wear it at all times except at work. At first

Arlene stayed a distance from me because she didn't want to be close to me if I got nasty comments from passersby. Later on, though, she accepted the change and was more supportive.

Also, in 1984 I ceased to answer the phone on Shabbos. From 1978 until 1984 I would answer the phone only but would make no calls on Shabbos. When I first ceased to answer the phone, this was much to my mother's chagrin. She used to call on Shabbos because outgoing calls from Dallas on Saturdays were cheaper than on Sundays. However, my mother came to accept the change.

In 1985 I took another job and decided that this time I would wear my yarmulke at work and take off all the Yontivs. Since I started the job in March, I first took off the seventh day of Pesach. The first two days were Shabbos and Sunday while the seventh and eighth days were on Friday and Shabbos.

The second night of Pesach in 1985 (April 6) was an interesting experience. Arlene and I went to the Seder of the family in whose house the shul was held. The patriarch of the family lead the Seder and he allowed no one else at the table to participate. He did all the reading and talking.

We began with the Kiddush, followed by the washing prior to the prayer over the vegetable (Karpas). This was followed by the breaking of the matzah. Next came the four questions. Why is this night different from all other nights? 1) On all other nights we may eat chometz and matzah, but on this night only matzah? 2) On all other nights we may eat many vegetables, but on this night maror? 3) On all other nights we do not dip even once, but on this night we dip twice? 4) On all other nights we eat either sitting or reclining, but on this night we recline?

The real beginning of the Haggadah is the answer to the four questions. The answer begins with "We were slaves to Pharaoh in Egypt." We at the table thought that we would continue on. However, after the head of the family read the first two short paragraphs, he said "Let's go back to the beginning." He repeated the first two paragraphs.

We continued two more paragraphs when again he said "Let's go back to the beginning." Again he read "We were slaves to Pharaoh in Egypt." He continued to read only two paragraphs at a time before returning to the beginning. This continued for two more hours. I already was getting impatient and I thought that Arlene would be lost to traditional Judaism.

After another half hour I finally couldn't contain myself. He again said "Let's *GO BACK* to the beginning." I gave very angry looks at the table and I whispered to someone "It's getting hot in here; and it's not the horseradish." The head of the family noticed my impatience and he asked "Irving, what's bothering you?"

I replied "I tried to contain myself but I just have to say something. Pesach is supposed to be a festival of freedom. But it's not a festival of freedom the way you're running this Seder. Why are we always going back to the beginning? Every minute it's *BACK TO THE BEGINNING, BACK TO THE BEGINNING, BACK TO THE BEGINNING.* Just what are you trying to accomplish by doing this? Why can't we just take it straight? We were already right at the point to have the meal and then you backtracked. As I said, Pesach is supposed to be a festival of freedom. But, instead of feeling free, I feel like a prisoner."

He just looked at me and said "I want you to know that I do this every year. You just don't know what we do because you haven't been here for our Seders." However, he didn't return to the beginning anymore. He continued at the point where we were to have the meal. After the meal he took the second half of the Seder straight. Everyone at the table was glad that I spoke up.

For the remainder of that Pesach he and I didn't talk to each other. He gave me the cold shoulder when we met at his house where shul was held. On the eighth day at his house I apologized to him for my outburst. I just grew impatient because I never had experienced such a Seder. He replied that he felt put down by correcting him in front of his children. He ended by saying "Maybe you don't need the lesson of our liberation; but they (his adult offspring) need the lesson."

Until 1989 the shul met at people's homes. Also, we met for a while at the Hillel House, the Heschel Day School and the Valley Child Guidance Center. Later on we acquired a house in Northridge and we were able to move into the house in April, 1989. We have been there ever since. In fact, I was the shul president when we acquired the house.

In 1993 I became the gabbai sheini (second gabbai). Here I would assist the gabbai rishon (first gabbai). A year later the gabbai rishon retired and I was elected to serve in his place. I remained in this position for seven years when I became first vice president. After a year, though, I was once again elected gabbai rishon. I served here until I declared retirement in 2004.

In 2006 I came out of retirement and ran for gabbai rishon. Instead, I was elected gabbai sheini and served in this capacity until 2016 when I once again was elected gabbai rishon. As of this writing, I continue to hold the position.

My Jewish observance has increased through the years. Beginning in 1985 when I bought new woolen clothes, I have had them checked for shatnez (the forbidden mixture of wool and linen). The Biblical prohibition states (Deuteronomy 22:11) "You shall not wear combined fibers, wool and linen together."

In 1986 Arlene and I had a son whom we raised religiously. He attended religious day schools throughout his school years and learned in yeshivas instead of attending college. Originally, his mother planned to have him learn in the Yeshiva for one year and then return home to attend college. When I visited him at his yeshiva in Israel in January, 2005, he said that he wasn't going to college. I gave him a congratulatory kiss and was happy that he wouldn't be making my mistakes.

I wondered how I would break the news to Arlene that we should keep him in Israel to learn. I called her and said that Tzvi does not belong with us. Instead, he belongs here and should continue learning in the yeshiva. I thought that I would get the argument of my life. Instead, she just said "OK."

Tzvi currently lives in Miami Beach, Florida with his wife and children. He teaches at the Yeshiva Middle School and does Kiruv (outreach) work. The tradition continues.

CHAPTER 5

PUNCTUALITY

This is the Internet's description of punctuality. "Punctuality reflects the integrity of a person. It indicates that he is brutally honest. He is honest to himself and in his commitment to others. When he has decided in his mind to arrive on time, he has stayed true to his own words."

Being on time means that one is respectful of the other person or group. Arriving late shows a lack of respect for the other person or group. In this regard one is saying that it's OK to be late. Let's look at it from a shul perspective. In the Talmud tractate Shabbos, page 127a, we read about precepts whose fruits one enjoys in this world and in the World to Come. One of these is early attendance at the house of study morning and evening. This also applies to early attendance to shul.

The shul needs 10 men to make a minyan (quorum). If no minyan is present, some of the prayers must be left out. These include the Barchu, the Kaddish, and the repetition of the Amida (silent devotion). What gets my goat is to see men coming to shul 40 minutes late and just now making a minyan when we are almost finished davening. In fact, the Gemara discusses tardiness in making a minyan. It says "When the Holy One, Blessed is He, comes to a synagogue and does not find ten men there, He immediately becomes angry. As it is stated, 'why is it that I have come and there is no man? I have called out and there is no one to answer.'"[11]

During the days of the Beis Hamikdash the Kohanim (priests) were divided into 24 groups to perform their watches at the Sanctuary. The incoming watch divided its bread in the north so it would be apparent that they were the incoming watch. The outgoing watch divided its bread in the south so it would be apparent that they were the outgoing watch.

The watch of Bilgah always divided its bread in the south whether the watch was incoming or outgoing. The Gemara offers an explanation why Bilgah and his watch were penalized. "And there are those who say that Bilgah's watch would

---

11 Talmud tractate Berachos, Artscroll, Chapter 1, p. 6b1, Mesorah Publications Ltd.

be tardy in coming to the Temple when it was its week to serve. As a result Yeshevav, his brother (his fellow Kohen), replaced him and served in his stead."[12] In addition, because of the tardiness of the watch, the alcove of Bilgah and his group of Kohanim was kept locked. This way they were forced to divide their bread from someone else's alcove. This was a humiliating blow to a group of Kohanim to not have access to their own alcove.

I get upset when we begin our services and a minyan isn't present. We are supposed to proceed to the first Kaddish after some of the introductory prayers. When a minyan isn't present, we normally move on. However, some want to wait while one or two more men are just coming into the shul from outside. If we wait for the late comers, they will have the attitude that we will always wait for them and then say the Kaddish.

During my tenure as gabbai I have instructed that we move on and continue until we get to the next Kaddish. When men of the congregation said to me that the few more men in the driveway will make the minyan, I often have responded "Yes, but they're not in here." With that we moved on with the service and the next Kaddish was said when we had a minyan.

---

12 Talmud tractate Succah, Artscroll, Chapter 5, p. 56b, Mesorah Publications Ltd.

A guest who was a Kohain came to shul for Shabbos and I offered him the Kohain aliyah for Shabbos morning. When time came for the Torah reading, he failed to show up for the Kohain aliyah. I thus had to call another Kohain. In fact, he came to the shul when the Torah reading was nearly completed. After greeting him, I asked what happened. He said that he couldn't get ready in time. As far as I was concerned, he should have made a greater effort to get ready in time to come for the Torah reading. On Shabbos morning the Torah reading usually begins an hour after the service has started.

At another time we had eight men on a Sunday morning, just two shy of a minyan. Our Sunday morning davening begins at 8:00 o'clock while Monday through Friday it begins at 7:00 A.M. Forty minutes later when we were almost finished davening, two men walked in to make the minyan. When we finished davening, I couldn't hold back. Without mentioning names, I publicly said that we start at a given time. I went on to say to the minyan that tardiness is rude, disruptive, disrespectful, and inconsiderate. In order to have a cohesive minyan, it's important to come on time and not when one feels like coming. Coming late means that one just doesn't care.

Later that day I received a WhatsApp message from the shul rabbi. I thought that I was going to get it. Instead he said "I understand that this morning you gave serious mussar (rebuke). Baruch Hashem (Blessed is the Name)." It felt good to have support.

If one wants to make excuses such as that they couldn't get ready in time; or they live too far from their workplace, I (most of the time) don't buy it. Prior to my retirement I lived 44 miles from my workplace. During the winter months on Fridays I still was the first one at the shul when the davening begins at 4:30 P.M. Thus, I feel that most excuses are invalid.

This is not to say that one doesn't have occasional extenuating circumstances. We all have them at times. A few years ago on a weekday morning I arrived 35 minutes late (7:35 A.M.) because I took a train from Dallas to Los Angeles and the train arrived at Los Angeles Union Station at 6:30 A.M., a half hour late. I then had to wait for my Uber ride to take me from downtown Los Angeles to shul in Northridge.

Upon arriving to shul I was greeted warmly by the rabbi and others. I apologized for being late and the congregation realized that this was a circumstance beyond my control.

Thus, sometimes tardiness is due to circumstances beyond our control. However, this shouldn't happen constantly. When going to shul, one needs to make every effort to arrive on time. After all, when one goes to his job, he makes every effort to get to work on time. The shul should be treated the same way. If one gets to work on time to please his boss, how about pleasing our Ultimate Boss by getting to shul on time? For many decades we have heard the expression "Jewish Standard Time" to signify that an event will begin later than the official time. As far as I'm concerned, there is no such thing. This phrase is just a saying for those who tend to excuse themselves because they don't have the self discipline to come on time.

Davening is starting. Let's not be late.

CHAPTER 6

WAITING

I detest waiting for anything. I don't like delays and get upset when I have to wait for someone or something that should have happened sooner. In the perspective of a shul I don't like when we are at the point in the beginning of the service to say kaddish and we have to wait for a minyan to come in. Where were the stragglers at the beginning? I might not mind waiting (2) minutes for the remaining men to come in and make up the minyan so Kaddish can be said. But, I have had to wait almost 10 minutes in the past and this is uncalled for.

The Kitzur Shulchan Aruch says that those who are present wait before saying Yishtabach until 10 adult men arrive.

They may wait before saying Yishtabach for close to half an hour; but they should not wait more than this.[13] I doubt that this practice is continued in our time, especially during the weekdays when the men eventually need to go to work. Shabbos and Yontiv might be a different story, but I never experienced a half hour wait to continue with Yishtabach. On Shabbos the longest wait I have experienced is 10 minutes; and even that drives me crazy.

This waiting reminds me of other times when I have had to wait when it wasn't my fault. I was in New York's Kennedy Airport where we were supposed to fly back to Los Angeles. We then were told that the flight was delayed. No reason was given.

No airline employee was at the gate. Thus, I tried calling the airline to see if someone would help. No one answered the phone. Here we all were waiting for some information as to when our plane would arrive. It turned out that the plane was originally supposed to fly in from Europe and then take us to Los Angeles. However, now we were told that the plane had mechanical problems in Europe and never took off.

---

13 Ganzfried, Rabbi Shlomo, Kitzur Shulchan Aruch, The Code of Jewish Law, Artscroll Series, The Kleinman Edition, Volume 1, pp. 164-265

It was hours later when the airline instructed Atlanta to fly a plane from Atlanta to New York and take us to Los Angeles. We were (6) hours delayed. And then, to top it off, the airline told us in their announcement "Thank you for your patience." What patience? Who can be patient in a situation like this? I certainly can't.

Returning to the shul scenario, I feel that if we wait for the late stragglers to arrive for Shacharis, they will have the attitude that we always will wait for them and they will always arrive late. I feel that we should begin Shacharis (where Yishtabach is) immediately after the Pezuki Dizimrah whether or not we have a minyan. This will show that we won't wait for late stragglers. They should care enough to come on time so we don't have to wait at all.

At our weekday Mincha davening we usually begin on time as we have a minyan at the designated start time. If the shul rabbi is present, and no minyan is present, he will make the call as to when we daven on our own. If he is absent, and no minyan is present, I will have us begin the Mincha davening five minutes before sundown. I then will have us daven Maariv 21 minutes after sunset. However, if a minyan is present for Maariv, I will have us daven right at sunset (or immediately afterwards) in order to keep the minyan intact.

The best-case scenario is when all come on time and no waiting is necessary. This shows derech eretz (good manners).

CHAPTER 7

WALKING TO SHUL IN HOT WEATHER

On Shabbos I walk to shul since we are not permitted to drive. I don't mind walking in the cold weather or when the wind kicks up a bit. There is one thing, though, that I can't stand. And that's walking to shul in the hot weather. Here I agree with Andy Rooney wholeheartedly.

Many will remember him and I guess some don't. Andy Rooney was an American radio and television writer who was best known for his weekly broadcast "A Few Minutes with Andy Rooney," a part of the CBS news program 60 Minutes from 1978 until 2011 when he passed away.

In his book titled "And More," Rooney writes an essay about hot weather. He says that he detests hot weather. That's easy enough for him to say in the middle of a heat wave, but he will say the same thing on the coldest day of the year.[14] So will I.

I remember some of the hottest days here in the Los Angeles area. We might not think that it's as bad as a severe storm, since much property is lost during the latter. However, in terms of the human spirit heat is worse.[15] In a hurricane or other disaster people work side by side to help each other. However, in the brutal heat, we don't find such camaraderie. In fact, heat has been known to cause irritation among people.

Our condominium complex used to have gas air conditioners that belonged to the homeowners association. Whenever a unit needed to be fixed, the association covered the expense. These gas units were not engineered to work in the heat that we get here. The refrigeration constantly went out. Suffering in that heat wasn't pleasant. The heating

---

14 Rooney, Andy And More, p. 121, Warner Books, Inc. New York, NY
15 Ibid., p. 122

& air conditioning company had to come constantly to fix our units.

A few years later when the repair technician came again, he said that the generator was trashed. It was beyond repair and the association wouldn't pay $12,000 to replace it. The association then lent Arlene and me electric window units. Although they were not designed to do the job that a central system can do, they were better than those gas air conditioners. A few months later the generators in all the gas units were trashed.

A few years later the CC&R's were changed and the association said that we could purchase our own units. Eventually Arlene and I bought an electric central air conditioner and it was money well spent. The unit worked much better than the gas units.

When I drive in my air conditioned car, I often pass by those who have to work outside in the brutal heat. These include those who are in construction or road repair work. My heart goes out to those individuals who have to suffer with these elements.

On a winter night on Shabbos I can bundle up in the cold weather. But in the hot weather what remedy is there? I can't stand walking home on Shabbos evening in the summer at 10 O'clock in the 90 plus degree heat. Then comes the next day when walking home from shul we're trapped in 100 to 105 degree heat. I often wish that we were permitted to drive to shul and back home on Shabbos in the summer months.

CHAPTER 8

A STORY MY FATHER TOLD ME

My father grew up in Berlin, Germany. He and his family attended shul on the High Holy Days and occasionally during the year. Across the street from their shul was a dairy restaurant. The restaurant was opened year round and the shades always were up. Thus, the customers could look outside and the street walkers could look in.

At one time in the year the shades were closed. When was this? Yom Kippur. The restaurant was open, but keeping the shades closed was the owner's way of letting the Jewish customers save face. These people would sneak in around the back and eat something to avoid suffering. Afterwards, they walked out through the back and made sure that no one from the shul would see them.

My father's family was not one of these people, but there was one thing that my father's father couldn't resist. That thing was smoking. He ushered in the shul during the High Holy Days. On Yom Kippur when there wasn't much foot traffic outside the shul, he went where no one could see him, pulled a cigarette out of his pocket, lit up, and took three puffs. He then exhaled heavily to avoid being detected by others. He performed this ritual a few times during Yom Kippur day. Somewhere along the way we all have our weaknesses. Even though my father's father was not very observant, he didn't ride the streetcar on Shabbos.

For a few years I had my weakness on Yom Kippur. I broke down and ate after the Musaph Kidusha. I did this from age nine through age 14. When I was 15, I decided that this wasn't right. From then on I have fasted the entire Yom Kippur. Also, for many years I didn't fast during the other fast days. However, when I did Teshuvah, I fasted on those days also.

Fasting is still very hard for me. I still do it although it gets hard after a long time without food and/or drink. The fast of the 10th of Tevet is the easiest since this is in the winter time and the day is short. The most difficult fast day is the 17th of Tammuz. This goes for over 16 hours. And besides, it's in the summer time with the unbearable heat. Tisha B'Av, however, isn't that hard for me since we begin the fast the night before. Therefore, when waking up in the morning, I'm already used to the fast.

During all the fast days the fasts are easy in the beginning. However, as time goes on, it gets harder. This is especially true in the summer. However, I don't give in. I try to remember that the fasts serve to do Teshuva and examine our ways.

CHAPTER 9

A LETTER FOR THE AGES[16]

The Ramban's letter (Rabbi Moshe ben Nachman 1194-1270) to his son admonishes him to stay away from anger, a serious character flaw. He says "Banish anger from your heart and remove evil from your flesh.[17] He goes on

---

16 Title of book with letter from Rabbi Moshe ben Nachman (the Ranban) to his son with commentary by Rabbi Avrohom Chaim Feuer
17 Feuer, Rabbi Avrohom Chaim, quoting the Ramban's A Letter for the Ages who quotes Kohelles 11:10, p.16, Mesorah Publications, Ltd., Brooklyn. NY

to instruct his son to speak gently to all people at all times. Even in tense situations when the atmosphere is charged with hostility, speak gently. Gentle words have even more force than crescendos of indignation.[18]

Rabbi Eliezer said "Do not be easily provoked to anger."[19] The commentator says that if one wants to refrain from abusing his/her fellow's reputation, he/she should not be easily angered.[20] If one is easily angered, he/she loses his/her ability to think straight. Perhaps forgetfulness comes from much anger.

Anger unsettles a person, causing him/her to act thoughtlessly and impelling him/her to aggressive behavior. When a wise person reflects on the fact that people are prone to anger, he/she strives to perfect his/her character in order to successfully moderate his/her passions.[21] King Solomon said "Do not be hastily upset, for anger lingers in the bosom of fools."[22]

Rabbi Shimon ben Elazar said "Do not appease your fellow when he is angry."[23] This teaches us that doing a good deed at the wrong time can actually do damage. If one tries

---

18 Ibid, p. 27
19 Pirke Avos, 2:1
20 Magriso, Rabbi Yitzchak on Pirke Avos, Me Am Loez, p. 104, edited by Rabbi Aryeh Kaplan, Maznaim publishing Corp. New York/Jerusalem
21 Lau, Rabbi Yisroel Meir, Rav Lau on Pirke Avos, vol. 1, p.276, Mesorah Publications Ltd.
22 Koheles 7:9
23 Pirke Avos 4;23

to appease his/her friend while he/she is angry, he/she might not pay attention to his/her words and might not even realize that he/she is trying to appease him/her. In fact, he/she might grow more angry.[24] It normally is a mitzvah to appease a friend when a wrong has been done. However, the timing is also very important. Otherwise such attempts could be counterproductive.

This was written because I basically am talking to myself. I have had anger issues throughout the years and have tried very hard to overcome them. Much of the issues go back to childhood and other times when I felt that I had been wronged. However, I'm working to realize that these issues happened long ago and it's time to move on. However, I'm dealing with these issues better than in the past. I try to remember from what King Solomon said "He who is slow to anger is better than a mighty man and one who rules his spirit than one who captures a city."[25]

I close this chapter with the closing paragraph of the Ramban's letter to his son. "Read this letter once a week and neglect none of it. Fulfill it, and in so doing, walk with it forever in the ways of Hashem, may He be Blessed, so that you may succeed in your ways and merit the World to

---

24 Magriso, op. cit., p. 210
25 Mishlei 16:32

Come that lies hidden for the righteous. Every day that you shall read this letter, Heaven will answer your heart's desires…Amen, Selah!"[26]

CHAPTER 10

LASHON HARA

Lashon Hara has been a weakness for a long time. I didn't know anything about the laws of Shmiras Halashon until I was in my 30's. However, through learning Torah and associating with the Orthodox crowd, I have been more successful in battling the desire to speak negatively about others. What also helped was to learn the writings about Shmiras Haloshon by the Chafetz Chaim[27] with my son. I'm not perfect by any means. But, I think I'm better at it now than decades ago.

---

[27] Rabbi Yisrael Meir Kagan (1838-1933)

Lashon Hara causes much pain to others. I should know because I caused much pain to others in the past because of it. The failure to guard my tongue came primarily from my own anger when I felt that someone wronged me. Lectures were given on it and I attended them. These lectures about lashon hara made me more aware of the ramifications of such speech.

Imagine why many friendships are lost or considerably damaged. Imagine why organizations (social or business) fold. It's a good chance that loshon hara was the cause. Who wants to part of a group or business organization whose members badmouth one another?

Decades ago in a lecture I attended regarding lashon hara, the rabbi[28] said that when it's spoken, three files are now opened. They are 1) the speaker of it; 2) the one listening; and 3) the one whom the lashon hara is about. When these files are opened, the Heavenly Court determines either one or all of these three should face punishment. All I know is that I don't want to face judgement.

Mark Twain was right when he said "Better to keep your mouth closed and appear stupid than to open it and remove all doubt." From King Solomon we learn "He who guards his mouth and his tongue guard his soul from many trou-

---

28 Rabbi Mendel Kessin, who spoke at Young Israel of Northridge in December, 1990

bles."²⁹ We also learn from King Solomon "Be not rash with your mouth and let not your heart be hasty to utter a word before Hashem. For Hashem is in Heaven and you are on earth. Therefore let your words be few."³⁰ Rabbi Akiba said "…The transmitted Oral Torah is a protective fence around the Torah; tithes are a protective fence for wealth; vows are a protective fence for abstinence; a protective fence for wisdom is silence.³¹

---

29 Mishlei 21:23
30 Koheles 5:1
31 Pirkei Avos, 3:17

CHAPTER 11

ARLENE

"A woman of valor who can find? Far beyond pearls is her value."[32] Such is the description is Arlene. She and I were married 40 years until her untimely passing. Since she passed away on Hoshanah Rabbah, I don't say "Stand by" in the shul in order to honor her memory. And besides, she actually didn't like it.

Beginning in September, 1976 she and I were part of the Bayit (house in Hebrew). This was an outgrowth of the Hillel group. The Bayit met Friday nights. Prayers were said over the candles, wine, and challah. Here is where I met her. I had been part of the Bayit for a year when Arlene began attending

---

32 Mishlei 31:10

in September, 1976. Before the session started, I commented to people about the one-pound steaks I occasionally would eat. She smiled and asked "Are you going to invite me for steak?" I said that I would think about it. At that time I had no particular interest and was dating someone else.

After a few weeks Arlene would be called on to light the Shabbos candles with the blessing. After the blessing over the candles we sang in unison the Kiddush for wine and the prayer for the challah. This was followed by the weekly Jewish topic of discussion.

In March, 1977 Arlene announced at the Bayit that she had a new boyfriend. We all congratulated her. I didn't realize until 10 months later that this was a dumb move on my part. In May, 1977, though, I asked if she would like to see a movie with me on the Sunday night of Memorial Day weekend. She actually accepted to go out with me. We saw Black Sunday starring Robert Shaw and Bruce Dern. Still, though, I had no real interest and afterwards didn't ask her out again until March, 1978, 10 months later.

We went to a party given by a Hillel member. At this time I began to be interested in her. I still didn't know why it took me a year-and-a-half to have any interest. Also, here is when I began to be more observant Jewishly (much to Arlene's chagrin) due to having been influenced by Rabbi

Ben and attending the Hillel minyan until it folded before Pesach, 1977. However, Rabbi Ben held High Holy Day services at the Hillel House that year which I attended and participated.

A few weeks after our March, 1978 date I asked her out to dinner. She asked "What night?" When I replied "Saturday night," she said "Ooh, I don't know. I'LL have to see." I reminded her that she had just gone out with me on a Saturday night. She replied "Yes, but I have a boyfriend. I can give you some Saturday nights and other nights, but not many Saturday nights." We went to dinner on a week night.

During our dinner conversation I brought up the hypothetical topic of whom I would like to marry. I said that I don't expect my wife to be Shomer Shabbos and to go to shul with me all the time. I just require one thing…a strictly kosher home. Arlene replied "No way Jose. I won't do that for any man." I then told her that she might change her mind some day and will fall in love with an Orthodox man and keep the kosher home. Again she replied emphatically "No way."

After the evening was over, I asked her if I could see her again other than in the Bayit. She said "Yes, but not always on a Saturday night." What was so uncanny was that in spite of her having a boyfriend, she always gravitated toward me at the Bayit. Shortly thereafter she and her boyfriend broke up.

I asked her out again and she asked what night. When I said Saturday night, she again said that she would have to see. "I thought you and your boyfriend broke up."

"We did," she replied. "But I have another one now."

"You sure didn't give me a chance."

"No, I guess I didn't."

"Are you and he serious?"

"I don't know."

I still asked her out. She said that Saturday nights needed to be planned ahead of time because of her boyfriend. Our next date was the evening of Mothers' Day 1978 which coincided with my birthday. We went to dinner and then to my apartment where I hosted the party, having invited some of the Hillel group to help me celebrate. Arlene gave me a book titled "Railways Then and Now," knowing my interest in trains.

Two weeks later I spent an in-Shabbos at the Yeshiva University of Los Angeles. After Shabbos I went to a party. When I saw Arlene at the Bayit the following Friday night, she said that she tried to call me that past Saturday night to say that she was available to go to the party with me due to her boyfriend having other plans. I apologized and said that I went to the party directly from Yeshiva University. Had I been home to answer the phone, I gladly would have taken her.

In mid-June Arlene and I were invited to a house warming party in my ex roommate's apartment. She was my date for that since this was on a Sunday. Shortly thereafter on a Sunday Arlene and I saw the movie "The End" with Burt Reynolds and Dom Deluise.

In July, 1978, now that my ex roommate was gone, I changed my kitchen to strictly kosher. I couldn't do this while he lived there because he was up tight about keeping a kosher kitchen although he agreed to it originally. When he left, though, I now could have a kosher home as I wanted for quite some time. When I needed to discard my old non-kosher dishes, Arlene agreed to take them. She came over and had dinner with me and I then helped place the old dishes in her car.

Also in July, 1978 I was invited to a party to take place on Saturday night, August 26. I asked Arlene far in advance to please go with me that one Saturday night. She said "OK. That one I'll do."

After I helped Arlene put the old dishes in her car, I drove us to the Hillel House for the student lounge event. People would socialize and enjoy each other's company. This time, however, Arlene and I were the only ones who showed up along with Marcie Nortel, the lady in charge. Both Arlene and Marcie knew each other due to being former members in the same chapter of the B'nai Brith Girls (BBG).

Since we were the only three there, we engaged in conversation. I told Marcie that Arlene wouldn't go out with me on a Saturday night because of her boyfriend, but went out with me all other times. I asked Arlene in front of Marcie if she is serious with him. Again Arlene said "I don't know." Marcie then commented to Arlene "You're not serious." And, while pointing to me, Marcie continued "If you were serious, you wouldn't be going out with Irving all the time."

I said to Arlene "One of these days I'm going to be your Saturday nighter. " "Ha hah," she said. "Funny."

"Who's joking?"

"You are and it's not funny."

"Well, you said you would go out with me to the Saturday night party in late August."

"Yes, I said that one I'll do. But you will never be my Saturday nighter."

"Well, we'll see about that."

I mentioned the issue of the kosher home. Arlene said

in front of Marcie "no way Jose. I won't do that for any man." "And I won't give it up for any woman," I replied. "So I guess we can't have anything. "No, I guess we can't," she replied.

The night before the August 26 party we were in the Bayit. A half hour before the Bayit event began, I took Arlene aside and told her that I didn't like the way she treated me. When I told her that I wouldn't want a wife like that, she fought back tears. I asked if she would rather be the next night with her Saturday nighter than to go to the party with me. She said "No, not particularly."

I let her know that on one hand she won't go out with me on a Saturday night. But on the other hand she comes into my place running it and bossing me around like we have been married for 10 years. I asked if she ever did that with other guys she dated. She didn't.

"You said that you won't keep a kosher home for any man," I said. "Well, I won't give it up for any woman. And if it means to have to lose you, so be it." Arlene almost cried. I said that I had worked too long and hard to have a kosher home and that I would be stupid if I let her or any woman come in my house and tell me I can't have it. Arlene fought back tears.

To conclude I told her that I was her real boyfriend. And if she didn't start treating me right, she would lose her real boyfriend. I also told her that I didn't know who else she was dating and didn't want to know. But I didn't like that whenever I wanted a Saturday night date with her, it had to be planned weeks in advance. She gently replied "It no longer has to be planned weeks in advance."

"What happened with your Saturday nighter?" I asked.

"I broke with him after our last date."

"Are you saying that I now can have it whenever I want it?"

"That's right," she said gently. "You can have it whenever you want it."

I waited a long time to hear that. I closed by saying that whoever married me keeps a kosher home. Arlene smiled and said "We'll talk about that later." I felt better now that we cleared the air.

A few Saturday nights later while on a date I said to Arlene "If I keep enjoying your company this much, I could want to keep you around. She said "OK."

"You know my one requirement," I said. She said what I wanted to hear for a long time. "I'll keep a kosher home." A week later we were engaged.

We were married on August 5, 1979 at The Sportsmen's Lodge Hotel in Studio City (the structure gone since 2021).

Arlene knew almost nothing about the practical aspects of a kosher home. Therefore I taught her. After a few months she got used to it.

Three years later I told her that I no longer was comfortable in a shul with no mechizah. I only sat with her at the traditional minyan so she could be comfortable. When I told her that I now was davening at the Chabad in Encino, she didn't like it because she always went with me on the High Holy Days to the traditional minyan at the Conservative shul. We were there together the last time for the High Holy Days of 1982.

In December, 1982 I got off the phone with Richard Macales. I knew him from the Orthodox Hillel minyan and he called to ask if I was interested in starting an Orthodox shul in Northridge. Arlene happened to hear the conversation. When I told her what Richard and others and I had in mind, she said "WHAT!? You're crazy. I'll have nothing to do with it."

On a Saturday night in June, 1983 Arlene came with me to Young Israel for our first meeting to elect officers. She cast her ballot for the offices, but still wouldn't daven there. In spring 1984 the Young Israel of Northridge had a general meeting. Arlene agreed to go with me.

Rabbi David Rue, our first rabbi, said that he heard that

some of the women didn't like the mechizah. He then suggested to the women who were present to design a new one as long as it was according to halacha. Arlene joined the other women to design a new one. Also, in the fall of that year, she attended High Holy Day services at the Young Israel of Northridge. Their services were held at the student union at California State University Northridge. I was happy to see her.

In 1985 Arlene began coming to shul for Shabbos Mincha in addition to coming on the High Holy Days. Here she began showing an increased interest in the shul. During this time we met in someone's house as we wouldn't have our own place until April, 1989. Arlene also joined us in 1985 for Shavuos. On the first night she stayed up with us all night learning Megillas Ruth.

In April, 1986 our son Tzvi was born. He was a beautiful addition to the family. At 2 ½ we enrolled him in nursery school at Emek Hebrew Academy. He stayed there through two of his middle school years. His last middle school year was spent at West Valley Hebrew Academy. Afterwards he spent all four high school years at Valley Torah High School. From there he spent several years in yeshivas in Israel.

During Tzvi's first year in yeshiva, he was able to convince his mother to cease working on Yontiv. Thus, in addition to Rosh Hashnah, Yom Kippur, and Pesach Seders, she took off every Yontiv. Shavuos 2005 was her first full Yontiv in shul (although she always took off the first day Shavuos). Also, she always took off on Simchas Torah. I was happy to have her with me for I now no longer felt alone on Yontiv.

From 1993 until her passing Arlene volunteered to host visiting yeshiva students for some of the meals. These students were here for the Summer Educational Enrichment Development (SEED) program. She cooked nice meals for the boys and they were happy to be given home cooked meals. Other families hosted them on other evenings.

In December, 2013 Arlene became very ill. I tried to help but without success. After many months of seeing doctors with no success, Tzvi called from Miami Beach and suggested that she take on more religious stringencies. One of these was to daven every morning and another was to cease wearing pants. She began davening every morning and ceased wearing pants. In January, 2015 Arlene got well.

In 2017 the shul sisterhood approached her and offered her the Kiddush coordinator position after the former one resigned. She accepted. She learned the ropes very quickly and ran the shul kitchen like clockwork. Also, she continued buying necessary foods and drinks for the Kiddushes (which she always did when she was not the coordinator).

Arlene passed away on October 20, 2019. At the time it coincided with Hoshanah Rabbah. She was a tzedekes who was a very sweet and kind lady and a world champion wife, mother, and grandmother. Her dedication to the Young Israel of Northridge was impeccable. She was always there to help set up for Kiddush and Shalosh Seudos (third meal in Hebrew). Due to her passing on Hoshanah Rabbah, I won't say "Stand By" on that day.

When visiting our grandchildren in Miami Beach, she always wanted to spend every waking moment with them. Since our visits were short, she didn't want to miss a minute.

May her memory be for a blessing.

EPILOG

I still am gabbai at Young Israel of Northridge and have held the post off and on for 32 years. I still enjoy giving out the honors and setting up for Shalosh Seudos on Shabbos afternoon. I try not to get annoyed anymore when people come late to shul. I remember the saying by Ralph Alpert (may he rest in peace), the main shul founder, "It's just as easy to be five minutes early as it is to be five minutes late."

I thank the Northridge Jewish community for its support since I lost Arlene. It would have been much more difficult to manage on my own. Their names appear on the dedication page.

ABOUT THE AUTHOR

I was born in Dallas, Texas, in 1948 — just a year after my parents came to America from Shanghai, China, where they found refuge after escaping Germany during World War II. My family's story has always reminded me of the strength and faith that carried so many through difficult times.

I grew up in a Conservative Jewish home where we observed the High Holy Days, Pesach, and Chanukah. My mother came from an Orthodox background, and my father did not, so our home was a blend of both worlds. From my earliest days in Hebrew school in South Dallas, I was drawn to Jewish tradition and the meaning behind our customs.

Over the years, I've continued to deepen my connection to Judaism. I serve as a gabbai, helping to make sure services and Torah readings run smoothly and reverently. It's a role that keeps me close to my community and to the heart of our faith.

In writing Confessions of a Gabbai, I wanted to share the experiences, reflections, and lessons I've gathered along the way — not as a tzaddik (righteous man), but as someone who's still trying to get there.

www.ingramcontent.com/pod-product-compliance
Lightning Source LLC
Chambersburg PA
CBHW050527100526
44581CB00009B/152/J